AF305038

SONGS OF SUPPLICATION

SONGS OF SUPPLICATION

Malathi V. Moily

Translated by
Geetha Sreenivasan

Illustrated by
Mohit Suneja

RUPA

Published by
Rupa Publications India Pvt. Ltd 2013
7/16, Ansari Road, Daryaganj
New Delhi 110002

Sales centres:
Allahabad Bengaluru Chennai
Hyderabad Jaipur Kathmandu
Kolkata Mumbai

First published in Kannada by Aasha Sahithya Maale 1995

ISBN: 978-81-291-2387-9

10 9 8 7 6 5 4 3 2 1

The moral right of the author has been asserted.

Typeset in Berkeley 10/15

Printed by Replika Press Pvt. Ltd, Haryana

To my beloved Sonia Gandhi ji,
Who is an epitome of renunciation; who shines bright in
the tapestry of the history of the Congress party and India;
who has inspired, at critical times, the Congress party
and the nation afflicted with complex conflicts; and who
has always lovingly guided the party and the nation with
humane, but revolutionary, reforms.

—Malathi V. Moily

Contents

To Bhramaramba, the Lustrous Mother [1]

You are:
The Primeval Energy[2], the Supreme Energy,
Both fruition and salvation;
The goddess—terrible and fierce;
You are *Bhairavi* the formidable, O Lustrous Mother!

You are:
The *Kali* of darkness, and of total deluge;
The blessed goddess of compassion;
The auspicious one of perennial bliss
You pervade the whole universe, O Lustrous Mother!

You are:
The Supreme Being[3], spouse of Shiva;
Both the volcano and the ocean of pity;
The illusion and profundity;
You are omnipresent, O Lustrous Mother!

You are:
The marvellous, and the indivisible
The meditation and supplication;
Both the prayer and the motivation;
You are my passionate dream, O Lustrous Mother!

You are:
The entire creation and the totality of beings;
The source of both suffering and bliss in the world
The Time and the Ocean;
You are my inner self, O Lustrous Mother!

You are:
The inert substance and the pure spirit;
The cause of both destruction and blessing;
Action and Dharma—the righteous path;
You are the kin of my soul, O Lustrous Mother!

You are:
The Supreme Principle, and the Universal Soul;
The Primeval Egg[4], and the Form Beyond;
Neither a beginning nor an end you have;
You are beyond everything, O Lustrous Mother!

You are:
The wise one and the ascetic;
Both the Form and the Formless;
The All-knowing and the Essence;
I have come seeking you, O Lustrous Mother!

---

[1]*Bhramaramba*: Another name of Durga or Parvati; both Kittel's *Kannada-English Dictionary* and Monier-Williams' *Sanskrit-English Dictionary* give 'lustre' as one of the meanings of '*bhramara*'. Hence, *Bhramaramba* is 'the Lustrous Mother.'
[2]Shakti: Energy personified as a deity, called by different names.
[3]Eshwara: Lord of all, Supreme Being; similarly Eshwari.
[4]Brahmanda: 'Anda' means egg; the whole universe is likened to an egg shape.

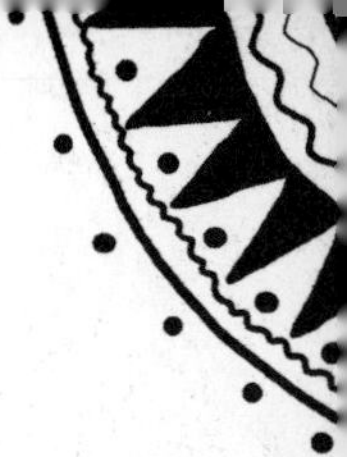

Hold My Hand and Lead Me On

Where are you hiding, O the Dark One?
Lord Krishna, come ye soon.
Without any pretences and playful pranks,
With your beatific smile, come ye soon.
I am tired, about to collapse, without your support.
Hold my hand and lead me on.

O friend of the lowly, *Dinabandhu!*
Come, Lord Krishna, Lord of the cowherds,
Govinda, come to me.
Loving child of Devaki, O Giver of Freedom,
O Mukunda the liberator, come to me.
Come, O Indestructible, *Achyutananda,* the truly Blissful,
Hold my hand and lead me on.

Loving child of Vasudeva,
O the Ruler of the whole world,
Beloved son of Yashoda, come, O Leader of the Yadavas;
The ever-shining mark of the Yadu-clan, come!
The ocean of all wealth, dweller with the goddess of wealth,
Come, O Player of the Flute,
O Slayer of the demon Mura,
Hold my hand and lead me on.

You the Little one of Nanda, O God in Human Form,
The play-field of Lakshmi,
Come, Lord, atop Venkata hill,
Lord of the Mount Govardhana, Patron of the world,
Slayer of the demon Madhu, Protector of your devotees,
O Liberator, Giver of bliss,
O Ranganatha, Lord of Pandharpura,
O Auspicious one, come unto me,
Hold my hand and lead me on.

You are the Lord of Lakshmi,
You lie on the primeval serpent,
You are the Lord of the whole world,
And the lord of speech,
You hold the Conch in one hand,
And the Mace in the other,
O Lord of Sesha Hill!

You are the Light of all lights, God of all gods,
You are Omniscient and Omnipresent,
The noblest of all beings,
O Supreme One, come unto me,
Hold my hand and lead me on.

O Lord of Lakshmi, the Ray of light for all!
O Lover of *tulasi*, the Liberator of all devotees!
O the One ever pure, the Ocean of compassion!
I bow to you and seek refuge in you.
Come unto me, without any pretences and pranks.
Hold my hand and lead me on.

6 · *Malathi Moily*

Nature

O Nature! Thou hast manifested here,
with beauty, incomparable.
Here, one finds charm incarnate
majestic, eye-catching, and divine;
Vernal glory, ecstatic, dances with abandon,
its peacock feathers, fully unfurled,
drawing colourful rangoli patterns on the earth.

The Vital Spirit has blossomed here,
myriad flowers, couple-coloured, singing in delight,
on the green, woolen carpet spread on the earth;
rows and rows of green chariots on the firmament,
sky-kissing trees in the dense black forests.

Mother Nature, dressed in colourful vestments here,
leaping cascades in gurgling bubbles here;
in the snow-covered splendour of the mountain peaks,
in the glorious Beauty, beyond words,
I stand here—engrossed, lost.

O Nature! Thou hast manifested here,
with Beauty, incomparable.

To the Companion

Across the seven seas are you and on this side, am I!
When you aren't near,
Void is my heart, void is my mind,
And the whole world too!
When I left you and came here, my heart weighed heavy;
But as soon as I remember your face,
it blossoms like a flower.
You are the vast ocean, and I am the fish within it;
But now, I'm a fish out of water.

Dull is the white-clad Nature in her snow-covering,
Dull and cold is my mind too, O friend.
Your talk, your flood of assurances—
They are my support when I feel lost.
Your words and acts—they are the guiding posts of my life;
Your deep voice the lullaby for my sleep.

You said everything would stand still in my absence,
including the sun, the moon, and the stars;
Look here, my friend, everything—
even the wind that blows across the seven oceans,
the birds and plants and trees—
everything is still and motionless.
If you aren't near me, my life-river is in turbulence;
I tell you, my friend, my existence depends on your presence.

Joie de Vivre

Full of excitement and hope, I left
for the European tour.
It is a sheer joy, in truth, to see Europe,
the most divine and wonderful place on earth.
The play of smoke, of jets and rockets,
crisscrossing the sky;

The swaying golden sheaves,
as far as the eye can see;
The farmers reaping their crops
with the machines that have wheels;
Rows of horizon-kissing mountains
and peaks of tall hills;
Lines and lines of shining buses and cars
speeding on the sleepy roads;

Eye-catching and beautiful
gardens with flowers fragrant;
The alluring curves
of blue-eyed belles;
Lush green farms of tall grass
stretching far and beyond one's eyes;
Smiling bunches of flowers,
peeping from crevices and pots;

The trolley went up and up sailing
To the summit of the snow-covered mountain.
My palm was ensconced
In the palm of my husband.
Without really daring to, I looked down,
Narrowing my eyes.
Immediately, I held my breath—
Beneath, the deep ravine gaped, threatening!

In Your Presence

Like a small child, hungry,
that yearns to see its mother,
groping in darkness, falling on the ground, frequently,
I have come to behold your Presence—
O my Father! Ayyappa! I seek refuge in you.

With legs tottering, heart beating fast,
Your name on my tongue, constantly,
My vision blurred with fatigue,
I have come to behold your Presence—
O my Father! Ayyappa! I seek refuge in you.

Coconut and ghee of cow's milk, I have brought;
Carrying the *irumudi* on my head,
Climbing eighteen stairways,
I have come to behold your Presence—
O my Father! Ayyappa! I seek refuge in you.

Neither in my thoughts nor in my dreams
had I believed I would be so fortunate
as to be in your presence.

In a great hurry, and full of anxiety,
have I come running to get your darshan;
I have come to behold your Presence—
O my Father! Ayyappa! I seek refuge in you.
I have come to behold your Presence—
O my Father! Ayyappa! I seek refuge in you.

Here, in your Presence, I stand with my head bowed;
I continue to look at you, my whole body all eyes;
My pen fails and words are inadequate to
describe your might;
O my Father! Ayyappa! I seek refuge in you.

I behold your Universal Form and I am thrilled;
My heart is full with your Form, I am truly blessed;
I behold your Form, radiant and divine,
and my life sanctified with your Presence.
O my Father! Ayyappa! I seek refuge in you.

Mother, I Surrender to You

In stones, in the hearts of your devotees,
Everywhere,
You have manifested yourself, Mother,
In your infinite mercy, protect me, O Mother!

I have come to you seeking refuge,
I stand before you, with bowed head;
I beg you, humbly and helplessly;
Open your eyes and look at me, O Mother!

You are there in my heart, every minute and every hour;
But, why are you invisible to me?
Bless me with your Vision, O Mother!

May my faith in you be ever firm;
May it be ever green, free from illusions;
Bless me with such faith, O Mother!
I totally rely on you, O Mother!

Mould

My heart empty, my speech muted,
And my eyes dimmed,
I search.

That miraculous mould,
that, with a vengeance, determined,
attempts to bind the broken links
between unknown persons
somewhere, in unknown places,
I don't know where
that miraculous mould is.
I search for it, here and there,
I dig up to see if I can find it;
Still, it eludes me.
Where? O where is that miraculous mould?

My heart tells me, my eyes can see,
that the power that can mould broken links,
O you, capable of taking any form that you fancy,
that power—rests only in you.

Sanctuary

Desires are numberless,
but despair is what I find everywhere;
My heart's yearning, in the form of tears,
flowing, has touched your divine feet.

I grew up as the loving child of your mercy;
And, as I grew, I became one with you.
I forgot my own separate existence,
And, I became a puppet of your playground.

Why did you breathe life into this puppet,
which plays as you wish it to play,
which dances as you desire it to dance,
and which exists according to your will?

Enough of this ordeal of fire for me,
What I need is only your sanctuary;
Enough of being bound to this earth,
if I am denied it by you.

Distant Mountain

Thinking that the distant mountain was smooth,
she approached it in a hurry to climb it;
Thinking that the mountain top was smooth,
she began her ascent, full of enthusiasm.

She climbed high, and she leaped excited;
But, as she went up she began to feel
that it wasn't as smooth as she had imagined,
that there were thorns and rocks aplenty.

She ignored them and continued climbing,
and, then, she confronted worms, insects and snakes;
still, undaunted, she continued her ascent,
but then, to her horror, she faced hungry tigers.
Though she was unnerved when she saw
those fierce beasts ready to devour her,
steeling her heart, determined to reach the top,
that appeared to her smooth and inviting,
she persisted, and reached the summit;
but, by that time, she had been wasted thoroughly;
a victim to the sharp teeth and nails of those beasts,
she had lost herself and her identity.

She realized, then,
that everything of hers had been plundered;
for a moment, she looked at them helplessly,
and, then—she leapt into the ravine beneath.

The Tulasi Garland

I drew, in my heart,
Your portrait.

I installed, neatly and cleanly,
your idol in my heart;
I admired, I worshipped
that idol in my heart.

I lit a lamp in my heart,
that shed light profusely,
to you—and to me.
I hid in my heart
your image
silently, secretly.

Blossomed in my heart,
like a blissful flower,
your love.
Now, it glories in your heart,
Firm and unshaken,
like a *Tulasi* garland.

That's the Way the World Goes

Yesterday's life is for yesterday;
Today's life is for today;
Life tomorrow is for tomorrow;
That's what one learns in life;
That's the way the world goes.

When you have, all come to you;
When you haven't, none comes near you.
When you have, all flatter you and serve you;
When you don't have, all mock you;
That's the way the world goes.

When one is strong and sturdy,
Relatives, friends, one doesn't need any;
When one is weak and helpless,
One cries for others, for succour;
That's the way the world goes.

We probe and list one's faults and failings
When one is alive;
But, we search for one's virtues and eulogize them
When one departs this world;
That's the way the world goes.

One is unaware there is nothing
That belongs to one, in this world;
We have to search for one, desperately,
Who is aware of this truth;
That's the way the world goes.

Altruism

My heart is full of pain and anguish,
For what reason I cannot fathom;
Since it is not certainly physical,
It has to be of the mind.

You cannot discover a trace of concern for others,
even with a microscope, in the animal called Man;
Mockery and shame are burning me like heated copper;
That's what pains my mind.

Words, of course, drip with honey;
but behaviour is pure hypocrisy.
It stabs my heart like a red-hot iron,
And that's what pains my mind.

If only human relationships, like a chain,
get linked with each other straight,
If the bud of altruism blossoms into smiling flowers,
then, nothing pains my body or spirit.

My Man

He is mine, different from all others.
No sooner would he step inside,
calling me sweet names, than he would cajole me;
and, raining kisses,
he would transport me into the world of Love.

He would freely chat with me,
and captivate my heart, completely;
Spraying drops of honey on my entire body,
he would revolve around me, like a bee.

He would melt down with just a glance of mine,
and would writhe in anxiety in my absence;
He would prattle with me, unabashed,
for hours and hours, unheeding of time.
He would patiently listen
to the joys and pains of my heart;
Singing lullabies and eulogies,
he would send me to sound sleep.

He would gladden my heart,
clearing off all my agony and anguish;
Making me float on sweet words,
He would enclose me with kisses.

Moving within my orbit,
embarrassing me in the presence of others,
signalling me to come out and join him,
he would imprison me in his arms.

Swimming joyously in the stream of love,
and floating carefree in the sky,
strolling in the world of dreams,
I would beam with pleasure, unaware of myself.

He would sulk if I frowned,
He would cheer me with his games,
He would get what he needed, like an obstinate child;
A rake, surely;
He is mine and mine only.

Heart Isn't a Ball of Flesh

Heart isn't a mere ball of flesh.
It's a drum that throbs continuously;
It's a spring of pains and pleasures;
It's an ocean of joys and thrills;
nay, it's a depth of endless agony;
Heart isn't a mere ball of flesh.

Heart is that,
which yearns and groans,
which understands another heart,
which responds to and hurts another heart;
nay, which assaults many others;
Heart isn't a mere ball of flesh.

Heart is,
a volcano of anger and enmity,
an oven of violence and vengeance,
a treasure of sympathy and consoling,
a structure that resounds with passions;
nay, it's indescribable in emotive words;
Heart isn't a mere ball of flesh.

Heart is that,
which shrinks in despair faced with mockery,
which gets hardened and protests against dishonour,
which sheds tears for the exploited poor women,
which goes all out in sympathy for orphaned children;
nay, which pities those who have eyes and still are blind;
Heart isn't a mere ball of flesh.

Heart is,
a clock that moves with regularity,
an eyelid that opens and shuts so quickly,
a geosphere that revolves round and round,
a river that flows with gentle sounds;
nay, a sea-wave that roars fiercely;
Heart isn't a mere ball of flesh.

Heart is that,
which thirsts for wealth and comforts,
which, with wealth, beams vainglorious,
which, losing wealth, screams and cries,
which, of others' wealth, gets envious;
nay, which considers large-heartedness wealth,
Heart isn't a mere ball of flesh.

Heart is,
that which yearns for the lover's union,
that which opens up with the lover's words of love,
that which blossoms with the lover's loving glance,
that which flies like a bird for the lover's kisses;
nay, that which forgets all in the lover's embraces;
Heart isn't a mere ball of flesh.

In the heart,
indomitable willpower is hidden,
the radiance of wisdom is found,
the bright lamp of all dharmas is lit,
the divine power is embedded;
nay, I can have salvation only when it stops;
Heart isn't a mere ball of flesh.

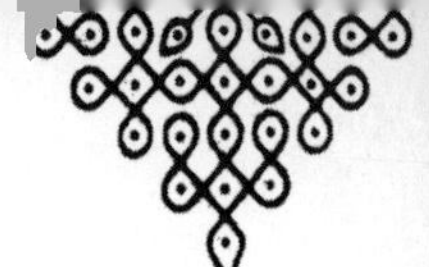

To Benaka

O Merciful *Benaka*[1] Have you really come to me, my
Master!
Have you, finally, come to me, my Master?
What have you seen in me, and for what reason have you
blessed me so,
to come to me and light up my life?

You are the *Ganapa*, the master of all Ganas,
and your face, crimson coloured, is so beautiful;
You are the *Ganapa* who loves *modakas,*
and you are pleased to come to me and bring me joy.

Your holy name is the guiding spirit of my life;
You are my very breath, and I owe my life to you;
You are the holy light to shed light on my life.

Why this silence, O *Vinayaka?*
Are you angry with me, O my God?
Stay in my heart eternally,
And, dispelling darkness, be my light, Father.

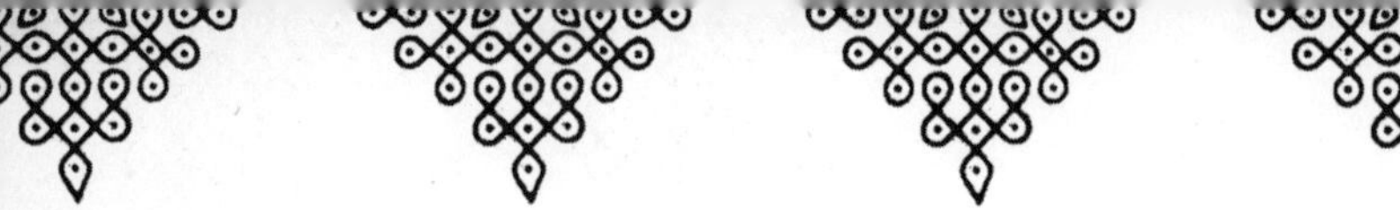

You are the *Kamadhenu*, the cow of Heaven,
that grants anything I ask for;
You are the *Kalpavruksha*, the tree of Heaven,
That gives anything I beg for;
Listen to my pleadings, O *Ganapa*,
Alleviate my pains, O *Benaka*.

The dust of your feet sanctifies my life;
Your hand of assurance brings contentment;
O Merciful *Benaka!*
Have you really come to me, my Master!

---

[1]*Benaka* is the Kannada equivalent of *Vinayaka* (Skt), which means an 'especial leader'; *Ganapa* is the short form of *Ganapalaka* (Skt), which means the one who protects all Ganas; *Modaka* (Skt) is a special sweet dish, held in one of Ganesha's hands. It is supposed to be a fond dish of Vinayaka.

34 · Malathi Moily

The Tender Bud

There was a time
when the entire environment was beautiful;
There was charm everywhere
and everything around was attractive.

There were smiles contented
on everyone's face;
In the cool breeze of green leaves
and the fragrance of jasmine,
Birds twittered happily
and golden moonlight spread everywhere.

A creeper put on new leaves
in the twilight aura;
A silver moon rose
in the sky-home of life;

It opened up all the three worlds to me.

The bud on the creeper of my body,
so pure and so precious like gold.

The Lord of the Seven Hills

O Lord of the Seven Hills!
Arise, O Lord, immediately,
Open your eyes and see me;
You are mercy, incarnate.

Crossing dense forests, I have come to you,
suffering and anxious;
Lift me up, Father, and comfort me.

Burning on the pyre of worries,
I have come seeking your solace;
Save me, Father, and protect me.

In my painful journey to you,
my heart is aching, my eyes full;
Are you standing there, with your eyes closed,
as if you cannot see the injustice of the world?

Like one of equanimity,
you are there, standing, unmoving;
You are the Spirit incarnate.

You, sleeping calmly on the soft coils
of the primeval serpent, Shesha,
As part of nature, are the Master of this Universe.
No other god is as large-hearted as you;
I seek your love, O God!

Vishnu, the protector of this world, lies, according to myths, on the huge coils of a serpent called Shesha, in the middle of an ocean of milk, *Ksheera Samudra.*

40 · *Malathi Moily*

The Enigma

Who answers it? Just who?
Without any answer, it has remained
An enigma.

The path of life isn't straight,
full of curves and turns and deviations;
the path forward is dim, dark;
Why? It remains unanswered.

When the confusing knots of life,
long sighs of pain and anguish,
throw me out, helpless,
The question 'why' remains unanswered.

Hearts that won't throb for others,
minds that won't think of others,
darkness enveloping my body—
Why? It has remained unanswered.

When the fierce fire of envy
burns me, body and mind,
I ask earnestly:
Why? It has remained unanswered.

When I am tired and exhausted
by the heat of the burning Sun,
a hard rock crushes me;
Why? It has remained unanswered.

When I climbed up as high as the clouds
marshalling all my limited strength,
I found the Earth laughing at me;
Why? It has remained unanswered.

When I was asleep, carefree,
an invisible hand hit me hard
and woke me up, trembling;
Why? It has remained unanswered.

When fireflies shone here and there,
I deemed them as light,
before lightning flashes revealed their true nature;
Why? It has remained unanswered.

When confusing knots and anxious sighs
leave me struggling for my breath,
desperately hoping for better times,
Questions remain without answers.

When, in the clear blue sky, white clouds floating,
suddenly, the clouds disappear,
revealing a dark naked sky,
The enigmatic questions remain unanswered.
Who has answers? Just who?

We Are...

We are—the backward people,
without gods, without a caste;
mention of our caste invites sniggers;
We are—the backward people.

Humble, with our backs bent,
voiceless and weak,
beaten up when we raise our voice,
We are—the backward people.

We don't belong anywhere;
We don't ever protest;
If we do, we are crushed brutally;
We are—the backward people.

We don't have any self-pride;
We don't have any self-respect;
If we have, it is burnt out;
We are—the backward people.

We also have dreams;
We have the courage to live;
But we aren't allowed to do so;
We are—the backward people.

They provoke those that lag behind;
They stab with their stinking tongues;
They wound with their sharp words;
For, they are—the forward people.

They ridicule with pointed pens;
They don't hesitate to stab from behind;
They blacken our faces, smilingly;
For, they are—the forward people.

They are butchers with stinging words;
They are slanderers, envious of us;
They are hypocrites, out and out;
For, they are—the forward people.

There is a volcano suppressed in these;
And, surely, it will erupt one day;
Now, these are blowing warning trumpets;
For, these are—the backward people.

46 · *Malathi Moily*

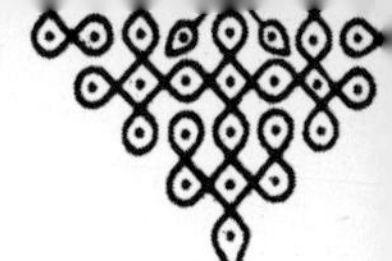

To Anjaneya

I am nothing, like a blade of dry grass;
You are *trivikrama*, occupying all the three worlds;
I am blinded in the presence of your *Vishwarupa*[1];
I have come, with trust in your feet, O Hanuma;
Don't falsify my trust, O God!
O Son of Anjanaa, Lord Anjaneya!

You are the great man, who cheered up Shri Rama,
When he was woebegone in Sita's absence;
Now, all the pain in my heart flows in the form of tears;
But where are you hiding,
O Lord Anjaneya, the son of Anjanaa!

You brought the signet ring to the husband of Sita,
What are you giving me, O Son of the Wind god?
Your holy feet constitute knowledge and wisdom for me,
Give me shelter in you,
O Son of Anjanaa, Lord Anjaneya!

O Hanuma, you are so mighty that you leapt over Lanka,
When will you help me to transcend the ocean of sorrow?
Heat of the wild fire is destroying my heart,
Come to me leaping, and extinguish the fire within me,
O Son of Anjanaa, Lord Anjaneya!

You brought from far *Sanjeevini* to Shri Rama's brother,
  Where are you now, when I am groping in darkness?
I am wounded, and I am blinded,
Come to me like a lamp and light my path in life,
O Lord Anjaneya, Son of Anjanaa!

To the spouse of Shri Rama, you brought the nosering,
Give me my nosering, and protect me, O *Muttutti Raya*[2]!
I sought your refuge, take me unto you and protect me;
I have had enough of this life, give me salvation, Father!
O Son of Anjanaa, Lord Anjaneya!

---

[1] *Vishwarupa:* The Form of god in which His omniscience is revealed.
[2] *Muttutti Raya* is another form of Anjaneya, or Hanuman.

I Bow to You, Gururaya

I have come seeking you, O Gururaya[1], don't send me away!
My will is weak, and I am caught in this material world;
Helpless I am, give me your assurance;
Won't you pity me, Gururaya? I seek refuge in you.

You have relieved the suffering of thousands;
Won't my desperate cries reach your ears?
Shri Hari was pleased with you,
Won't you be pleased with me?
Won't you pity me, Gururaya? I seek refuge in you.

Friend of my soul! Your compassion is endless;
Anchor my life that is drifting rudderless.
You are the One who knows what I need;
Won't you pity me, Gururaya? I seek refuge in you.

I shall ensconce you in my heart
And worship you with tulasi leaves,
Bathing you with milk, and Vedic chants;
Amidst all these that you love, I shall be a small part;
Won't you pity me, Gururaya? I seek refuge in you.

Your eyes have the radiance of a thousand Suns!
I see light in your eyes for me, desperate as I am;
Your eyes assure me of your loving protection;
Won't you pity me, Gururaya? I seek refuge in you.

Eternal Truth you are, my very breath you are!
I am ignorant of how to please you and worship you;
I swear I beg you only for salvation;
Won't you pity me, Gururaya? I seek refuge in you.

---

[1]*Gururaya* refers to Shri Raghavendra Swami, the great saint of
Karnataka who lived in the 18th century. Many miracles are ascribed
to him.

The Enemy Within

You are the enemy of yourself, not I!
Pluck out and discard the Evil in you;
Cleanse your mind of all hatred, and be free;
Make your heart-temple clean and pure;
I am not your enemy—you are.

Do not set fire, extinguish that fire in you;
Put off the fire of hatred that has enveloped you;
Put off the fire of enmity and anger in you;
Cleanse your heart of envy, and become human;
I am not your enemy—you are.

Do not boil in anger, do not be consumed in anger;
Do not stamp and scream in anger, and surrender to it;
Anger will get hungrier and will devour you;
Burn out that anger and be in peace;
I am not your enemy—you are.

Be free from pretences, don't look down on any one;
Do not be vain, vanity is unclean;
Vanity of wealth, vanity of authority,
None of these lasts long; virtues alone last;
I am not your enemy—you are.

Do not ridicule one's lineage, do not mock others;
Do not spread rot in the name of clan or caste;
Not God but man created clans and castes;
If you don't realize this truth about clans,
I am not your enemy—you are.

Give up ego and envy, and cultivate amity;
Don't be a victim of vanity, conquer it;
Don't be an enemy of anybody, don't hate any one;
Be large-hearted in this beautiful world;
I am not your enemy—you are.

Why Don't You Uplift Me!

Why don't you consider me your child, O Krishna,
and uplift me!
I will sing your paeans, come to me sporting;
You are not small—you are the Master of the Universe.
Your face is charming, your form all intelligence;
Sweet notes coming from your flute are captivating.
Where are you, Krishna? Where are you?

My tears have dried up, wearied is my body;
My joys and my sorrows—all belong to you.
I plead with you, I beg you humbly,
I am afraid, kindly console me.

I offer you the sweet-smelling sandal paste,
I worship you with flowers and *tulasi*[1] leaves.
You, adorned with the *Kaustubha*[2], are the ocean of mercy;
Consider me your child, O Krishna, and uplift me!

---

[1]*Tulasi*: A highly medicinal plant, considered dear to Krishna. It is grown in a pot in most Hindu homes.
[2]*Kaustubha*: Name of a precious gem worn on the chest by Krishna. This was got when the 'ocean of milk' was churned by the gods and demons. The Sanskrit word means 'that which pervades the whole universe'.

56 · *Malathi Moily*

You Are Omnipresent

You are boundless! You are everything
And You are everywhere!
The Sun, the Moon, and the galaxies of stars—
All exist because of you;
You are pure, complete, the highest Joy,
the Supreme Creator,
You are eternal, immeasurable, unequalled,
beyond everything.
You embody the vastness of countless oceans;
You possess the radiance of innumerable Suns.
You are beyond Time and Imagination, beyond any ends;
You are everything...boundless,
And You are everywhere!

In the echoes of the trees swaying in the wind,
In the sacred rituals and practices in front of the fire,
In the charming white clouds floating in the sky,
In the raindrops pouring down from the sky,
In the waves of roaring seas and flowing rivers,
You are everywhere...boundless,
And You are everything!

Immutable, free from falsehood,
And matchless Ocean of mercy,
Ever Pure, Truth personified,
And Treasure of mercy,
You are the Protector in distress, You are the closest kin,
Worshipping you is the path of salvation for me.
You are eternal and stainless; You are Truth personified;
You are everything...boundless;
And You are everywhere!

I have the illusion that I throw light on you
with endless lamps;
But You are the one that gives light to the whole Universe.
You are the Energy
found in the earth, sky, rivers and oceans.
Become the Light of Wisdom for me,
drowned in ignorance;
You are everything...boundless;
And You are everywhere!

Light Up My Path

I cannot see the path, it's enveloped in darkness;
Show me light, O Mother, and lead me on.
You are the First Cause of everything, the Creator,
You are the part of all forms of being;
The firm Earth and the flowing Water,
Wisdom and Ignorance,
Death and Eternity—all these are Your forms, O Mother!
The fire that burns and the water that flows,
The wind that blows—all these are Your forms, O Mother!

You know everything and You understand everything;
But why don't You understand my innermost heart?
Aren't You aware of my heart's pain?
If You won't, who else can protect me?
Even if You don't have any thoughts of me,
My thoughts are always centred on You.

There is none but You for me; You are everything for me;
Fulfill my heart's desires and give me peace of mind;
If not, free me from all these.

Look! I will now decorate You
And worship You with devotion;
Turmeric paste for your cheeks,
Kumkum for your forehead,
Sandal water and flowers—Jasmine, *Mandara, Suragi,*
Sampige, Davana, Kedage—all these I offer You.

O Mother! Giver of everything auspicious and good!
Eradicator of all sorrows! O Noble *Sharvari*!
Ruler of all the three worlds! Light up my path.

Salutations to Manjunatha

I bow to you, O Manjunatha!
O the benefactor of the poor!

I beg you, O cheerful and virtuous One!
Reassure me, You remover of one's fears!
O Ascetic! Wielder of the axe!
I bow to you again and again.
You are *Gangadhara,* one who holds Ganga
in one's long hair;
You are the eternal lover of Gauri!
I bow to you again and again.

I have suffered in this world of birth and death;
I have no peace;
Assure me of peace, O Hara;
You free one from this world's fears.
O Lord! Free me from sins and evil deeds;
O wielder of the trident! Bearer of the Moon on your head!
I bow to you again and again.

Weak and humble am I, You are the most generous of all,
And I submit to you.
Light up the abode of my heart,
And grant me peace and contentment, O Father!
O Lord of the Three Worlds, blessed with three eyes!
I bow to You again and again.

In my very breath and sighs, when I am awake or asleep,
In the very blood that flows through my veins and nerves,
I meditate on your name, sacred and magical;
O Joy Incarnate, dressed only in coarse skin-cloth!
I bow to You again and again!

I submit to You that I have suffered slander and malice;
I submit to You that my faith in you is unshakeable;
Give up Your anger and Your hauteur, O Moon-crested!
I bow to You again and again.
Lighting incense and lamps, offering You
bilva leaves and *tumbe* flowers, bathing You
with ritual water and milk, I worship You.
You love drum-sounds; You are absorbed in meditation;
Your face is ever-cheerful; You are the spouse of Parvati;
O You, the ocean of endless compassion!
I bow to You again and again.

Have You Come Here to See Me Suffering?

O my patron goddess!
All around me there is pitch darkness,
And in this dark night, I cannot see my path;
O Ocean of compassion!
Won't you show compassion to me?

Like the tireless sea waves
Lashing against the seashore, again and again,
I bow to your feet at every step of the road.
Tears, uncontrollable, stream down from my eyes,
But you refuse to recognize their intensity;
Whether it is devotion or distress that I experience,
Lift me up, O Lustrous Mother, and protect me.

The struggle and confusion of this life—
It is all a game for you;
But I am defeated and wasted, O Puppeteer!
Grant me an auspicious sign of strength and courage.

My Dear Friend

Seven seas away from each other,
You there...
I am here...
When you are not here,
My heart is nothing...
My Mind is nothing...
This world is nothing...
When I sailed apart from you, my heart felt heavy,
When I think of your face, Like a flower my heart
blossoms,
You are like an ocean...Inside there, I am a fish
Like a fish taken out of water...I am now.
Lifeless she is, covered with snowfall, in a white clad sari...
O! Nature
Like a sheltered snowfall, my mind has become,
My dear Friend!
Your words flood me with buoyancy...I wait
in anticipation for your words that hold me.

Your ways, are my support...
Your depth of voice is like a lullaby in my sleep...
You said to me,
"Without you, the sun, the moon and the stars
have vanished..."
Look here my friend, the seven seas, the wind,
the plants and the trees have vanished too.
If you are not close to me, my life is in a shamble.
I say my dear friend, I am nothing without you!

My Mother

Mother, your remembrance to my memory's extent,
This image was created;
Hair parted to one side with a bright smile on a moonlit
face,
At the centre of your forehead was the red Sindoora[1],
Like the champa flower, your long nose had a ring of ruby
and pearl,
A precious white stone of small earrings in your beautiful
ears,
Like the full moon light spills, so was your tender smile,
Everlasting pure and gentle was your beautiful tender smile,
Your favorite hue of orange coloured soft sari, you draped
With emerald green bangles on your arms,
Your neck, shaped like a white conch,
adorned the Mangalya[2]
With black beads that shone,
Thick long tresses rested and spread on your back,
On your striking toes, silver toe-rings I remember,
Soothingly sleeping, I remember, on your warm lap,
Your lotus shaped palms, caressing my back, I remember,
You embracing me and loving me I remember, when I
tripped on my little feet,

My naughty self, you watched and softly screamed at me, I
remember,
You cajoled me, I remember, when I fought with my elder
sister and came crying,
Sitting on a footstep, you sat looking at my pranks with a
giggle, I remember,
In the evening, you, sitting in the courtyard, I remember,
next to the tulasi[3] abode,
You with me, holding my hand while climbing a rock, this
sweet memory, I remember,
Sitting on a horse cart, watching you, I remember, beside
my father,
You saw of me, only three spring times, I remember,
Four people carried your dead body, harshly and bitterly, I
remember,
Mother, all this, in my breathing breathe, imprinted in my
heart,
Your fresh memories, I remember.

––––––––––––––––

[1]*Sindoora*: Red powder made of turmeric, usually worn by married
Indian woman.
[2]*Mangalya*: A locket given by an Indian husband to his wife, at the
time of marriage.
[3]*Tulasi*: A sacred herbal plant, especially worshipped by married
Indian women.

The Sprout of My Womb had Sprouted

Like this, there was a day,
A splendid day,
Everywhere there was beauty,
Everything was lovely,
Everybody smiled,
With a dancing gait,
An ever green of calm breeze,
Scent of the jasmine,
Birds joyfully chirped songs,
The Full moonlight spread gold brightly,
In the evening of twilight, a creeper bloomed,
My eyes saw new light, my body electrified,
In the vastness of my life, a Star was born.
In my awareness, the cosmos I discovered,
The sprout of my womb had sprouted a pure gold child.

Acknowledgements

My sincere and heartfelt thanks to the following people
for making this book possible:

My husband, Dr M. Veerappa Moily; my daughter, Hamsa Moily,
and Shri K.R. Kamlesh.